Original title:
Paths Less Traveled by Wolves

Editor: Jessica Elisabeth Luik
Author: Paulina Pähkel
ISBN HARDBACK: 978-9916-86-441-8
ISBN PAPERBACK: 978-9916-86-442-5

In Silence They Tread

In shadows deep where whispers rest,
The silent journey of the blessed.
Footfalls light on paths unknown,
In twilight's hush, they walk alone.

Veiled by night, their secrets keep,
In stillness pure, the woods they sweep.
No echoes trace their silent flight,
In the realm where dreams ignite.

Stars above, a distant guide,
In silent grace, the veils they bide.
Through ancient groves and forest bed,
In silence, softly do they tread.

Through Untamed Lands

Across the wild, the fierce winds blow,
Through untamed lands where shadows grow.
A path unmarked, a quest unknown,
Into the wild, where dreams are sown.

Mountains rise and valleys dip,
The heart of nature's fierce grip.
Untamed lands of jagged stone,
Each step leads to realms unknown.

By roaring tides and still lagoons,
Through sunlit days and starry moons.
The spirit wild, the soul unplanned,
Wanders through each untamed land.

In the Company of Trees

Beneath their branches, whispers weave,
In the company of trees, we grieve.
Ancient trunks reach to the sky,
In silent peace, the leaves do sigh.

Roots entwine in earthen bed,
In their shade, the world we shed.
Stories old in bark are told,
In the company of trees, we hold.

Among their limbs, the spirits play,
In sunlit beams and twilight's sway.
With trees so wise, our hearts we ease,
In the timeless company of trees.

Forest Reveries

In the woodlands deep and fair,
Dreams take flight in softest air.
Mystic shadows dance and weave,
In forest reveries, we believe.

Emerald light through canopies,
Whispers float on gentle breeze.
A tranquil haven, heart's reprieve,
In the depths of forest dreams, we achieve.

Nature's secrets softly spun,
In the glow of setting sun.
Magic stirs the woodland seas,
In the spell of forest reveries.

Echoes of Solitude

In the quiet of twilight's embrace,
Where shadows weave their gentle lace,
A whisper of wind through the trees,
Stirs memories carried by the breeze.

Alone beneath the starlit dome,
Thoughts wander far from hearth and home,
Each silence speaks, a soft, sweet song,
Of days now past and nights so long.

Footsteps echo on a lonely lane,
Hushed whispers of forgotten pain,
In solitude, the heart finds peace,
As echoes of the past release.

Nocturnal Paths

Moonlight dances on the forest floor,
Casting shadows, whispers lore,
Softly treads the traveler's feet,
On paths where dream and reality meet.

Owl's gaze from branches high,
Guardians of the starry sky,
In the hush of the midnight air,
Secrets flourish everywhere.

Mysteries woven in the night,
Guide the seeker with gentle light,
Nocturnal paths, a sacred maze,
Where the soul with wonder stays.

Silent Wanderings

Beneath the canopy of stars,
Silent wanderings leave no scars,
Through meadows bathed in silver light,
Whispers carry through the night.

Dew-kissed grass and moonlit streams,
Cradle softly woven dreams,
In the stillness where shadows play,
Silent hearts find their way.

Boundless skies and endless spaces,
Silent wanderings find their places,
In the quiet, where whispers blend,
Solace found, journeys end.

Into the Whispering Pines

Through the grove of whispering pines,
A trail of dreams and ancient signs,
The rustle of each emerald leaf,
Echoes tales of joy and grief.

Sunlight filters soft and gold,
Through boughs that have a century old,
In this forest, whispers yearn,
For the secrets they discern.

Footprints on a mossy bed,
Leads where countless pathways thread,
Into the whispering pines I go,
Where the soul's true colors show.

Daring the Unknown

To venture forth where shadows creep,
Into realms where mysteries seep.
The brave embrace both fear and thrill,
Traversing paths up the daunting hill.

With heart ablaze, they face the night,
Eyes aglow in the dim starlight.
A whispering wind guides their quest,
Each step a dare, a conquering test.

Through mist and gloom, they forge ahead,
By daring hope and courage led.
In every echo, strength they find,
For in the unknown, paths unwind.

Night in the Wilderness

Stars alight, the night begins,
The wilderness, its secrets spins.
Ebon tapestry, moon so bright,
Caresses the world in gentle light.

Whispers weave through ancient trees,
Echoes ride on midnight's breeze.
Creatures stir in the twilight's hue,
The forest wakes, life anew.

A campfire flickers, shadows play,
Stories shared till break of day.
The wild sings its ancient tune,
Underneath the watchful moon.

A Wilderness Tale

In forests deep, where time stands still,
Myths and legends weave their thrill.
Amidst the pines and hidden streams,
Nature's grandeur, like vivid dreams.

Echoes of the past remain,
In rustling leaves and falling rain.
Soft whispers of a time long gone,
Find life anew with each new dawn.

Wolves' howls sing of olden days,
Their haunting, wild, timeless praise.
A story told by earth and sky,
Of ages past that never die.

Veiled Canopy

Beneath a veil of leaves so green,
A sheltered world, a hidden scene.
Canopies in layer upon layer,
Whispers of adventure in the air.

Sunlight dances through the fronds,
Nature’s tapestry responds.
Cicadas hum in rhythmic cheer,
The forest's song both far and near.

Mysteries held in each leaf's fold,
Secrets of the wild untold.
Veiled by branches, high and low,
An untouched realm where spirits go.

Twilight Wanderings

The day bids farewell, the night softly greets,
As twilight lingers where land and sky meet.
Shadows grow long, and whispers take flight,
Guiding our steps through the encroaching night.

Stars start to sparkle, painting the dome,
Each one a beacon, leading us home.
With every footstep, our hearts find a song,
In twilight's embrace, where we both belong.

The moon, a guardian, watches above,
Bathing the path in soft light and love.
Crickets sing praises, the wind tells a tale,
Of twilight wanderings where dreams set sail.

Secret Groves

Deep in the forest, where few dare to tread,
Lie secret groves where magic is spread.
Whispers of ancients in leaves overhead,
Mysteries hidden where sunlight does shed.

Vines intertwined, creating a veil,
Hollowed-out trees, telling old tales.
There in the quiet, secrets come clear,
In secret groves, where the heart sheds its fear.

Rays of light dance on dew-covered leaves,
Stories untold in the bark they weave.
Nature is silent, yet speaks to the soul,
In secret groves, where we feel whole.

Shadows in Motion

Under the starlight, shadows come alive,
Moving with grace, they silently strive.
Dancing on walls, with a rhythm unheard,
In shadows in motion, no sound is preferred.

Through moonlit meadows, they twist and they sway,
Silent companions who never betray.
Merging and parting, an endless romance,
Captured in moments, a shadowy dance.

Whispers of winds guide their silent quest,
In shadows in motion, they never rest.
Eternal dancers, with no one to see,
Living their lives in pure mystery.

Lost in the Thicket

Twisting and turning, the path disappears,
Lost in the thicket, amidst ancient fears.
Whispers of branches, secrets they keep,
In shadows and foliage, the memories seep.

Footfalls muffled on moss-covered ground,
Everywhere silence, not a single sound.
Eyes wide in wonder, searching for light,
Lost in the thicket, embraced by the night.

Hope is resilient, a glimmer of gold,
In the heart of the forest, courage takes hold.
In the tangled embrace, we find our own way,
Lost in the thicket, through night into day.

Sable Spectrum

In the depths of night it sprawls,
A canvas void of stars' bright calls,
Whispers float amidst the sheen,
Of darkness deep, unseen.

Midnight hues that coil and weave,
Twilight tales we scarce believe,
Sable dreams in shades profound,
Where secrets of the past abound.

Nebulous and velvet cloak,
Veils the world in mystic smoke,
Swirling tendrils, dark, obscure,
In its folds, our hearts secure.

Silent symphonies, shadows play,
Till the break of dawning day,
Unveils the night's celestial theme,
Awakens us from sable dream.

Reflections in the Timber

Sunlight dances on the leaves,
Nature's ballet amidst the eaves,
Timber whispers ancient lore,
Stories from an age before.

In the stillness, shadows cast,
Echoes of the timeless past,
Majestic trunks that weathered time,
Stand as poems in silent rhyme.

Emerald crowns in breezes sway,
Guardians of the dawning day,
Their reflections, memories we see,
In the forest's living sea.

Softly tread the woodland floor,
Hear the echoes, seek no more,
For in the timber’s soft embrace,
One finds a sacred, quiet place.

Forest Anomaly

In the heart of mossy green,
Lies a realm unseen, serene,
Where whispers of the wind can tell,
Of magic in the woodland fell.

Arcane echoes fill the air,
Phantoms dance without a care,
Mystery in roots entwined,
In shadows secrets are enshrined.

Luminescent fungi glow,
Casting eerie light below,
Foliage with a sanguine hue,
Warns of tales both old and new.

Venture forth with cautious tread,
Through the paths the ancients led,
In the forest, weird and wild,
Nature’s enigma, undefiled.

Whims of the Wild

Beastly howls through canyons ring,
Songs of nature free to sing,
Wild whims in moonlit glen,
Echoes call to hearts of men.

Leaping through the meadows bright,
Creatures dance in pure delight,
Boundless spirit, untamed grace,
Revel in this sacred space.

Beneath the stars, a covert glance,
Life's eternal, primal dance,
In the wilderness, wild and free,
We find our ancient reverie.

Let the wild reclaim our soul,
In its freedom find us whole,
In the whispers, fierce and mild,
We are children of the wild.

Courageous Strides

In twilight's subtle, fleeting grace,
We march with heart, a steady pace.
Through trials faced and fears denied,
We conquer all with Courageous Strides.

Beneath the stars, a guiding light,
We grasp at hope through darkest night.
With every step, though world divides,
We mark our path with Courageous Strides.

In whispers soft, our spirits soar,
We brave the storm, forever more.
For strength in us forever bides,
As we embark on Courageous Strides.

Mysterious Forest Hues

In shadows deep and verdant green,
Lie secrets hidden, yet unseen.
Where whispers call and darkness brews,
Behold the Mysterious Forest Hues.

The canopy of emerald leaves,
A cloak of nature, mystery weaves.
Through twilight paths that we peruse,
We wander through Mysterious Forest Hues.

With every step, a silent tale,
Each rustling leaf, a whispered veil.
In nature's grasp, where magic strews,
We lose ourselves in Mysterious Forest Hues.

Enchanted Forest Ways

Where fairies dance on moonlit beams,
And rivers weave with silver gleams.
A world of wonder, time obeys,
Within the Enchanted Forest Ways.

The trees alive with ancient lore,
They sing their songs forever more.
In twilight's maze, where dreams do sway,
We'll linger in Enchanted Forest Ways.

With every breath, a spell is cast,
As moments merge and shadows last.
In realms unseen, our hearts do stay,
Engulfed in Enchanted Forest Ways.

Feral Divergence

In wild expanse where nature reigns,
Life's essence flows through endless veins.
Where instinct calls and heart refrains,
Unleashed begins our Feral Divergence.

Through untamed lands where freedom's born,
We break from ties, no longer worn.
With primal pulse and spirit's surge,
We venture forth in Feral Divergence.

Beneath the skies, vast and immense,
We find our path without pretense.
Unto the wilds, our souls converge,
Embracing life in Feral Divergence.

The Road Less Roamed

In shadows where the dense woods loom,
A path unknown, a quiet tomb,
With leaves that whisper ancient tales,
Where only bravest heart prevails.

Step by step through twilight haze,
A wanderer in nature's maze,
Each footprint on the mossy ground,
Echoes of a world unbound.

Branches weave a secret song,
Guiding through the dusk so long,
Every turn a newfound thrill,
In silence, heartbeats still.

Moonlight casts a silver veil,
On a path that none can trail,
Mysteries in every stone,
The road less roamed, alone.

At journey's end, the sky unfurls,
Revealing life's uncharted pearls,
For those who dare to roam unknown,
Find treasures in the twilight zone.

Veering into Mystery

Beyond the fields where daisies play,
Lies a world where shadows sway,
A silent call to those who hear,
The whispers of the land so near.

With each step, the air grows thin,
A chill that seeps beneath the skin,
The forest breathes a hushed intrigue,
Veering into a mystic league.

Candles flicker on the breeze,
Guiding through the ancient trees,
Every rustle, every sigh,
Hints at secrets tucked nearby.

Stars above in silent pact,
Illuminate the unmarked tract,
A journey where few choose to steer,
Into the heart of twilight's sphere.

In the stillness, truths unwind,
Treasures of the wandering mind,
For through the veils of half-seen dreams,
Lie answers to the heart's own schemes.

Among Hidden Trails

Amidst the underbrush so dense,
Lies trails concealed without pretense,
A wilder path for souls that seek,
The whispers of the forest's speak.

Through twisting vines and fern-clad nooks,
With unseen streams and quiet brooks,
A dance of shadows leads the way,
Among hidden trails, feet stray.

Birds in chorus guide the ears,
Through grounds untouched by human years,
A symphony in green and brown,
Nature's secrets, primal crown.

The canopy of leaves above,
Shields a world of whispered love,
Where creatures roam and spirits dwell,
In whispers of a timeless spell.

At journey's end, a clearing found,
Bathed in sunlight, wrapped around,
Among hidden trails, hearts align,
With the endless flow of time.

The Feral Way

In wild plains where grasses sway,
Runs a path untamed, away,
The scent of earth and sky entwined,
A call to leave the known behind.

With every step, a bond renewed,
The feral way, the soul pursued,
No boundaries to fence the heart,
In nature's realm, a world apart.

The wolves that howl, the dusk's deep hue,
Echoes of a life so true,
In tattered cloth and bare-skin feet,
The feral way, where earth and spirit meet.

Mountains rise and rivers wind,
An endless journey, undefined,
Through sunlit days and starlit nights,
A trail of pure, untamed delights.

In freedom's grasp and nature's grip,
The traveler finds a kinship,
For on the feral way, souls find,
The wild within, the untamed mind.

Wolves in Seclusion

Beneath the restless midnight sky,
Silent shadows track their flight,
Through forests deep where secrets lie,
They wander into endless night.

Their howls an echo in the breeze,
A chorus that the wind repeats,
A symphony for ancient trees,
As solitude's embrace they greet.

The moon, a sentinel above,
Illuminates their cloaked domain,
In seclusion, wild hearts move,
Through darkness, they remain unchained.

Among the pines, a hidden dance,
Yet fierceness softens to a trance,
A moment’s peace within their glance,
The wolves in seclusion find their stance.

In shadows cast, they roam unseen,
Their spirits free, forever keen,
Through solitude, their paths serene,
In twilight’s cloak, a feral dream.

The Enshrouded Trek

Footsteps echo in the mist,
A path concealed, yet they persist,
Through shrouded woods where shadows twist,
Embarking on an endless quest.

Fog engulfs the towering trees,
Whispers ride the spectral breeze,
Lost in time, with hearts at ease,
They navigate the mysteries.

With eyes alert, through trails unseen,
They chase the truth in twilight's sheen,
Each step a bond, their souls convene,
A journey steeped in the serene.

The trek unfolds with every stride,
Beyond the realms where fears reside,
With courage as their only guide,
Through realms of dusk, they walk beside.

Enshrouded paths, an endless rhyme,
Their spirits free, transcending time,
In veils of mist, the path they climb,
A pilgrimage both vast and prime.

Beneath Moonlit Canopies

Beneath the moon's ethereal glow,
The canopies in twilight show,
A haven where the wild things go,
In shadows cast, a mystic flow.

Enchanted woods, a silver hue,
The night's embrace, a world anew,
In silence deep, they pass through,
A journey steeped in dreams come true.

Each star a witness to their flight,
Through realms of dark and realms of light,
Beneath the canopies so bright,
Their spirits soar, an endless height.

The whispers of the ancient trees,
Are songs that ride the midnight breeze,
They wander where their hearts at ease,
In moonlit realms, their souls release.

In twilight's cloak, their essence bared,
A unity in nature shared,
Beneath moonlit canopies, they dared,
To roam the night, undaunted, spared.

The Wolf's Veil

In misty veils where twilight weaves,
The wolves find solace, hearts reprieve,
Through shadows cast by moonlit eaves,
Their spirits roam the night to cleave.

An ancient call that stirs the night,
A haunting hymn that takes its flight,
In moon's embrace, their forms alight,
In veils of dusk, their souls unite.

Eyes aglow with wisdom old,
Through paths untold, their stories told,
In unity, their hearts unfold,
A legacy through night's behold.

The forest whispers secrets deep,
Through silent watch, their vigil keep,
In veils that through the darkness seep,
Their bond with nature ever steep.

In twilight's hush, they find their grace,
Through veils of dusk, they set the pace,
In nature's fold, their rightful place,
The wolves in veil, a sacred space.

Elusive Shadows

Beneath the moon's soft gentle glow,
In places only dreams can show.
Where shadows flit and whispers creep,
Silent secrets, shadows keep.

They dance on walls, they twist and turn,
In hidden corners, where night does burn.
Elusive whispers, secrets told,
In darkness, mysteries unfold.

They stretch long in the twilight's touch,
With silent grace, they never rush.
In every crevice, every nook,
Their silent sway, a phantom look.

The dawn will chase their forms away,
But in the night, they come to play.
With silent feet, and voiceless stance,
They lead us in their quiet dance.

Adventure in the Twilight

In the twilight's purple embrace,
We sought adventures, face to face.
With every step, a world anew,
In silence, we our courage drew.

The stars above began to wink,
As night and day in balance sink.
Through forest paths and rivers wide,
We journeyed on a timeless tide.

With lanterns lit by firefly beams,
We wove through midnight's silent seams.
In whispers carried by the breeze,
We trailed the shadows through the trees.

The horizon's colors began to fade,
Yet our spirits never swayed.
In twilight's hold, we found our quest,
Adventure lit within our chest.

Secrets of the Canopy

High above, where the eagles soar,
An emerald sea, a secret door.
In the canopy, life intertwines,
In whispered leaves, the forest shines.

Branches weave a tale unknown,
A fortress where the wild has grown.
With every rustle, every breeze,
The secrets dance among the trees.

In shadows deep, the night birds call,
Where ancient songs around us fall.
Whispers of the wise oak tree,
Share secrets of the canopy.

The sunlight filters, soft and warm,
Painting the forest in a charm.
Beneath the green, a veiled sight,
In nature's heart, a hidden light.

Twilight Mysteries

When day gives way to twilight's hues,
The world takes on a different muse.
In shadows long and stars' first light,
The secrets whisper through the night.

A gentle breeze that softly stirs,
In twilight's dusk, the night prefers.
With every sigh and whispered breath,
The mysteries evade certain death.

The moon ascends with silent grace,
Casting shadows on Neptune's face.
In twilight's arms, the secrets lie,
Beneath the stars that light the sky.

In every shadow, every shade,
A story written, softly laid.
The twilight mysteries unfold,
In night’s embrace, the tales are told.

Savage Serenity

In wild embrace, the tempests howl,
Nature's wrath, yet calm endows.
Fierce and tranquil, hearts disarm,
Serenity cloaked in savage charm.

Waves that crash, yet softly sing,
Peace within the storm they bring.
Ripples dance on waters wild,
A paradox, nature's child.

Lions roar, yet in their eyes,
Starlit dreams of silent skies.
In the roar, a whisper found,
Savage calm, the world unbound.

Mountains pierce the sky with might,
Stillness in their towering height.
Strength and grace in each ascent,
Power with serenity bent.

Through the chaos, find the peace,
In savage realms, calm won't cease.
Balance in the wild and free,
A savage, serene decree.

Whispers in the Undergrowth

Leaves rustle secrets in the night,
Hidden realms, 'neath pale moonlight.
Mystic whispers, softly speak,
In forest heart, the echoes seek.

Branches shield the ancient lore,
Timeless tales and something more.
Roots that coil in silent dance,
In undergrowth, a fleeting glance.

Shadows whisper, spirits near,
Nature's voice, so pure and clear.
In each rustling, stories blend,
Whispers in the green extend.

Flowers bloom with fragrant breath,
Silent witnesses to life and death.
Petals listen to the winds,
Undergrowth where time rescinds.

In the hush of nature's fold,
Whispers timelessly retold.
Through the green, the secrets flow,
In the undergrowth, hearts will know.

Moonlit Trails

Underneath the silver glow,
Pathways gleam where shadows flow.
Moonlit trails that weave and wend,
Through the dusk, where dreams ascend.

Silent steps on ancient stone,
Guided by the night alone.
Stars that wink in knowing grace,
Moonlit trails a sacred place.

Mystic whispers in the breeze,
Melodies of twilight ease.
With each step, the stories glide,
Wisdom walks the moonlit tide.

Crescent beams that light the way,
Softly kiss the path's display.
Journey through the twilight's veil,
Magic on the moonlit trail.

Dreams unfold where shadows fall,
Echoes through the night, a call.
Moonlit trails of silver trace,
Guiding hearts in twilight’s embrace.

Silent Footprints

On the sands where memories fade,
Silent footprints, journeys made.
Whispers of the past remain,
Etched in time, a sweet refrain.

Silent steps on paths untrod,
Boundless stories, feet have plod.
Echoes of a life unseen,
Footprints in the dawn serene.

Footfalls on the earth so still,
Carrying tales of heart and will.
Every step, a silent verse,
Of joy, of sorrow, and the terse.

In the hush, the prints unfold,
Ancient tales that time has told.
Silent footprints, paths of old,
Mysteries that life has polled.

Trace the silent steps of yore,
Feel their essence, their encore.
Silent footprints on life's shores,
Speak in whispers, evermore.

Mystic Creeks

Beneath the shadowed canopies, we seek,
A world of whispers where the willows speak.
The water's edge, a tranquil heart, it beats,
A symphony that calls through mystic creeks.

The silken sun slips through the emerald lace,
Its gilded touch on surface ripples trace.
In secret corners, where the lilies grow,
Mysteries of ages softly flow.

Whispers of wind through ancient pines unfold,
Secret tales of treasures yet untold.
Lost in the cadence, where the river bends,
Time's gentle current, here, transcends.

The sky above, a tapestry of blue,
Mirrored in the creek, a wondrous view.
Wanderers tread softly, led by dreams,
In the soothing hush of flowing streams.

Into the Timbered Unknown

Dense with shadows, the timber calls us near,
A realm where echoes gently pierce the ear.
Paths untrodden, veiled in twilight hue,
Guide us onward, to the brave, the true.

Whispers of leaf and branch above our heads,
Tell stories of those who once dared to tread.
In this sacred grove, we seek what's shorn,
The essence of nature, reborn, adorned.

Each step upon the moss a silent plea,
To hold in balance, what has come to be.
In the timbered unknown, we cast our fate,
And thread the needle of nature's gate.

Through shadowed umbra, bright the spirit's fire,
Carved by journey's edge, our own desire.
Here lies the heart of wild, undistressed,
In the timbered unknown, we find our quest.

Furtive Moves

In still of night, the silent steps begin,
Through moonlit paths where secrets thinly spin.
Shadows deepen, flutter in their grooves,
We walk the night with cautious, furtive moves.

Beneath the stars, our hearts afire, they beat,
In quietude, the world below our feet.
A touch of mystery in each hushed breath,
Against the stillness, life's whispered depth.

Veiled in twilight, hidden in plain sight,
We dance the steps between the day and night.
Each stride a promise, held in shadows' keep,
In furtive moves, the night our secrets keep.

The murmured dreams of yet uncovered deeds,
Through silent moves, the heart of night it feeds.
With stars as guides, our paths entwine and weave,
In stealthy dance, beneath the moonlit eve.

Beyond Trails Familiar

We leave behind the paths that we have known,
Venturing where the wanderer's heart is shown.
Beyond trails familiar, we cast our sight,
Seeking realms hidden from daylight's might.

The horizon calls with whispers of the new,
Uncharted lands where dreams and courage grew.
Each step we take on the earth's embrace,
Beyond old trails, we forge a fresher pace.

Mountains rise, their peaks to kiss the sky,
Valleys deepen where the echoes lie.
We tread with wonder where the wild things roam,
Beyond familiar trails, we find our home.

Mysteries await where the path is less,
In every twist, a chance to reassess.
With open hearts, our journey intertwines,
Beyond old trails, new destinies define.

Echoes Beyond the Meadow

Whispers of the willow, softly in the breeze,
Crickets sing a lullaby, nestled 'neath the trees.
Stars begin their vigil, across the twilight skies,
Echoes of the meadow, in the moon's soft rise.

Flowers in their slumber, dream of morning dew,
Ripples on a pond, where evening shadows grew.
Owls in silent flight, call to the distant night,
Echoes in the meadow, till the dawn's first light.

Veil of mist descending, on fields of emerald green,
Secrets of the night, in the starlight seen.
Footsteps fade away, as the twilight grows,
Echoes from the meadow, where tranquility flows.

Woodland Chronicles

Tall trees whisper tales, of ages long gone by,
Leaves that danced in sunlight, now in shadows lie.
Brook that murmurs softly, speaks of ancient lore,
Woodland chronicles, hidden at its core.

Deer tread softly, in the dappled light,
Birdsong heralds day, dispelling the night.
Paths wind ever deeper, where the ferns grow tall,
Woodland chronicles, echo in the fall.

Bark rough with stories, of seasons old and new,
Canopy of wonders, in a sea of green and blue.
Each step uncovers, a page that's seldom read,
Woodland chronicles, where the Earth is fed.

In Quest of Silence

Journey through the forest, where the quiet dwells,
Footsteps hushed by pine, in nature's silent wells.
Echoes of a heartbeat, blend with whispering leaves,
In quest of silence, where the spirit grieves.

Mountains rise in stillness, to the sapphire sky,
Rivers carve their paths, where the silence lies.
Mossy stones hold secrets, in the cold, calm hush,
In quest of silence, amidst nature's blush.

Twilight brings communion, with the stars above,
Silence speaks in wonder, tales of boundless love.
Rest within the stillness, as the night unfolds,
In quest of silence, where the heart beholds.

Moonrise Over Meadows

Silver light of moonrise, bathes the meadows wide,
Glistening on the grasses, where shadows gently slide.
Stars in silent chorus, gather in the night,
Moonrise over meadows, a tranquil, gentle sight.

Breezes weave a story, through the flowers bright,
Crickets lead the chorus, in the soft moonlight.
Paths of light and shadow, where the fireflies gleam,
Moonrise over meadows, like a waking dream.

Fields of endless whispers, in the silver hue,
Capture hearts and wishes, as old dreams renew.
Magic in the stillness, where the night abides,
Moonrise over meadows, where the soul confides.

Wilderness Whispers

Through the timber and under leaf,
Nature’s wisdom speaks in relief,
Silent murmurs echo far,
Guiding souls through morning star.

Rivers carve the ancient tale,
Mountains stand where winds prevail,
In the hush of twilight’s call,
Wilderness reveals it all.

Beneath the canopy’s green light,
Time stands still, a mystic sight,
Whispers grow as shadows stow,
Secrets of the wild bestow.

Among the pines and mossy stones,
Soft whispers turn to ancient tones,
Echoes of the earth’s deep past,
In the wild, our roots are cast.

So listen close and heart will find,
Wilderness speaks to open minds,
In the whispers, life unfurls,
The voice of nature, ancient pearls.

Unknown Horizons

Beyond the known, where sky meets sea,
Horizons call to you and me,
A venture into depths untamed,
Mysteries and dreams unclaimed.

Stars align in celestial dance,
Guiding us through limitless expanse,
Every wave a whispered clue,
To worlds beyond our shaded view.

Footsteps on a path unknown,
Carved by winds and waters flown,
We journey through the mist and night,
Towards the dawn's expanding light.

Eyes see far beyond the shore,
Mind imagines ever more,
Horizons stretch, inviting gaze,
Into the unknown's boundless maze.

Embrace the call, let spirits soar,
Unknown horizons forevermore,
Seek the edge and find the way,
To where dreams and secrets lay.

Veiled Landscapes

In the mist where visions fade,
Landscapes hide in twilight shade,
Veiled by secrets, whispered low,
Worlds within that softly glow.

Mountains loom in ghostly form,
Valleys sleep in silent calm,
Through the gauze of dawn’s embrace,
Veiled landscapes show their mystic grace.

Trees stand tall, their shadows blend,
With the night that never ends,
Silent murmurs fill the air,
Mysteries unveiled, everywhere.

Rivers flow in twilight’s sheen,
Reflecting dreams of what's unseen,
Beneath the veil, the heart can see,
The soul of nature’s mystery.

Walk the paths, the mist shall part,
Revealing truths held close to heart,
Veiled landscapes, ancient, wise,
Open to receptive eyes.

Strange Trails

Wander down the paths unknown,
Strange trails where wonders are shown,
Every turn a story untold,
Where dreams and visions unfold.

Footprints mark a journey's start,
To places hidden, maps depart,
Each new step, a mystery found,
In strange trails, where we're unbound.

Echoes of the past we trace,
On these trails through time and space,
Whispers from the earth and sky,
Guide us where the secrets lie.

Through the forest, by the stream,
Strange trails weave like vivid dreams,
In the unknown, courage grows,
Where the heart and spirit flow.

These trails lead to endless lore,
Strange yet familiar to explore,
Journey on, let soul prevail,
Through the magic of strange trails.

Secret Tracks

Beneath the whispers, earth-bound cracks,
Ancient roads, hidden acts.
Time's footprints, faint but sure,
Tales of yesteryears, pure.

Veiled by shadows, winding ways,
Enigmas of forgotten days.
Soft echoes in the evening's fold,
Unveiled stories, bold.

The moonlight mirrors what was passed,
Secrets held, yet not the last.
Each pebble, a keeper's call,
Mysteries for one and all.

Stars align, reveal the lanes,
Flowing through life's quiet reins.
Paths unseen, yet clearest tracks,
Bound in lore, none it lacks.

Into dusk, the journey bends,
Where the known and hidden blend.
Secret trails under skies,
Where history softly lies.

Magical Murmurs

In twilight’s glow, a whisper sings,
Magic in the air, it springs.
Soft incantations in the breeze,
Mystic voices through the trees.

Moonlight silvers, forest deep,
Secrets kept in nature’s keep.
Elves and sprites in hushed delight,
Dancing shadows in the night.

Waves of wonder lap the shore,
Ancient spells forevermore.
Crystal waters, secrets tell,
Enchantments where old spirits dwell.

Starlit heavens, endless charms,
Mystery in their open arms.
Every whisper, a spell's embrace,
Magical murmurs in this place.

Dreams arise in silent mists,
Where every heartache finds its tryst.
Hidden realms within the sight,
Of magical murmurs, pure and bright.

Phantoms of the Night

Midnight tolls with eerie chimes,
Echoing through the endless times.
Spectral forms in moon's embrace,
Haunting glows on mortal's face.

Shadows drift with silent breath,
Veils of life and depths of death.
Whispered names in starlit air,
Phantoms gathered, unaware.

Ethereal in pale moonlight,
Lurking just beyond the sight.
Ghostly hands reach into dreams,
Weaving through the night's faint beams.

Ancient souls with stories vast,
Bound by chains of lifetimes past.
In the night, their spirits tread,
On pathways of the silent dead.

Eclipsed by dawn's brightening ray,
Phantoms slowly fade away.
Yet in darkness, they confide,
Endless, in the night, they bide.

Journey Through Shadows

Winding paths where darkness lies,
Silent as the midnight skies.
Treading softly, fears unfound,
Shadows whisper all around.

Lanterns flicker, light and fade,
Casting forms where shadows played.
Each step closer to the heart,
Of the shadows' secret art.

Through the veil without a sound,
Mysteries in darkness bound.
Eyes that see beyond the sight,
Guide you through the endless night.

Echoes of a distant call,
Mirror shadows on the wall.
Footsteps blend and pathways wind,
In shadows' depths, the truths we find.

Till dawn breaks with golden hue,
Shadow's journey starts anew.
In the light and in the dark,
Journeys leave their lasting mark.

Forgotten Trails

Upon the paths where shadows creep,
Memories lie in whispered sleep.
Lost are the tales of yesteryears,
Faded by the ancient fears.

Footprints etched in weathered stone,
Silent voices, overthrown.
Twilight weaves a shroud so pale,
Veiling the forgotten trail.

Each step echoes past's embrace,
Ghostly figures, time’s slow pace.
In the hush of evening’s wane,
History’s echoes call again.

Leaves of autumn, crimson gold,
Tell of secrets left untold.
Rustling whispers in the night,
In the shadows out of sight.

Through the mists of time we tread,
Following where brave hearts led.
Seeking stories left behind,
On the trails we hope to find.

The Veiled Journey

Upon a road, half-hid from sight,
Blanketed in misty light.
Winds of change the wayward guide,
Through the journey, far and wide.

Veils of fog in silver light,
Lead us through the endless night.
Step by step, the path unfolds,
Mysteries of life it holds.

Whispered dreams like shadows fall,
On this road that calls to all.
Silent whispers from the dusk,
Lure us forth, a gentle thrust.

In the quiet, in the calm,
Where the night wears twilight's charm,
We wander through the silent mists,
With hopes and dreams entwined in twists.

Guided by the stars so sly,
Lighting up the midnight sky,
The veil lifts, the path is clear,
On this journey, love is near.

Among the Untamed

In the heart of wilds unknown,
Nature claims its ancient throne.
Beasts and whispers, fierce and free,
Tell their tales to you and me.

Underneath the moon's bright gaze,
In the forest's dark embrace,
Echoes of the wild untamed,
Call to those who dare, unclaimed.

Rivers rush and mountains soar,
Carving paths through earth's deep core.
Songs of nature, wild and bold,
Speak of stories ages old.

Beneath the canopy of green,
Worlds of wonder can be seen.
Fearsome, graceful, wild and pure,
Life's great dance in forms demure.

Here among the untamed lands,
Nature's law forever stands.
Harmony in harsh domain,
Life and death in endless chain.

Secrets of the Wilderness

In the wilderness, secrets lie,
Hidden from the naked eye.
Whispers of the ancient trees,
Carried on the gentle breeze.

Through the dense and shadowed brush,
Nature speaks in a sacred hush.
Every leaf and stone and stream,
Holds a part of earth’s great scheme.

Mysteries beneath the veil,
Woven in the fox’s trail.
Secrets whispered in the night,
By the owl’s ghostly flight.

Morning dew on spider’s thread,
Glistens where the wild have tread.
Marking where the secrets pass,
Nature’s wisdom, deep and vast.

In the heart of green so wild,
Rest the secrets luring, mild.
To those who seek with pure intent,
Wisdom of the land, content.

Questing Shadows

In twilight's grasp, shadows creep,
Searching lands where secrets keep.
A dance of dusk, a sullen sweep,
In silent woods, the shadows leap.

Paths unknown and questing shades,
A labyrinth where daylight fades.
Ancient voices call and cascade,
Guiding steps through darkened glades.

Underneath the moon's cold stare,
Ghostly figures fill the air.
Wandering with a haunted dare,
Midnight's cloak they proudly wear.

Eternal dark, a boundless sea,
Whispers of eternity.
Shadows quest, forever free,
In a realm of mystery.

Cool breezes stir the hidden night,
Silent as a raven’s flight.
Veil of secrets dark and tight,
A world beyond our mortal sight.

Beyond the Beaten Path

Wander where no feet have roamed,
Through lands that time has never known.
Mystic woods and peaks uncombed,
In shadows, secrets are intoned.

Tranquil streams, a silent call,
Where age-old trees stand broad and tall.
A hidden world within the thrall,
Beyond the path, we dare not fall.

Stars that guide when all seems lost,
Guiding through the seasons' frost.
Nature’s arms, a bridge uncrossed,
Leading where no soul exhausts.

Rivers of wisdom, winds that mend,
Each step forward, forevers blend.
Unseen realms around the bend,
To where the beaten paths must end.

Leave behind the worn-out track,
Into the unknown, no looking back.
Here, courage packs within your sack,
A journey on fate’s untrodden rack.

Whispering Pines

Silent whispers through the air,
Pines that murmur, tales they share.
Ancient secrets, ghostly fair,
In their shade, a world laid bare.

Softly rustling in the breeze,
Lullabies among the trees.
Nature's echo, forest's pleas,
Guardians of eternal seas.

In their shade, where shadows fall,
Songs of old do gently call.
Wisdom wrapped in nature's thrall,
Pines that whisper, standing tall.

Through the ages, they remain,
Witness to the sun and rain.
Pines that hold the past's refrain,
Watchful over hill and plain.

Underneath their boughs we tread,
Listening to voices, long since dead.
Whispering pines where dreams are spread,
Cradling thoughts within their bed.

Fog and Fear

In the mist, the shadows wait,
Fog that cloaks a hidden fate.
Steps that echo, paths of slate,
Piercing through the midnight late.

Ghostly forms that drift and weave,
Cloaked in secrets they conceive.
Eyes that watch, though you perceive,
Unseen hands that never leave.

Fear resides in every fold,
Tales of woe and legends told.
Chilling air, a gripping hold,
Dread that whispers, dark and bold.

Lost in fog, the mind does tear,
Searching for the light to bear.
Echoes from a distant lair,
Fog and fear, a timeless snare.

Courage found in heartbeats strong,
Guided by a distant song.
Through the fog, though nights are long,
Brave the fear and right the wrong.

The Untrodden Route

Along the path of whispers lost,
Where shadows play and time's the cost,
Feet tread lightly, hearts anew,
A world unclear but beckoning too.

Through brambles thick and valleys deep,
Where silence clings and memories seep,
The untrod way, with secrets sewn,
Each step a story, each trace unknown.

The wind it talks of ages past,
Of lovers' trysts and spells long cast,
With every turn, a mystery breaks,
In twilight's glow, the spirit wakes.

The stars unpin from heaven's cloak,
With each breath, the midnight spoke,
A pilgrimage, alone, profound,
To realms where dreams and truths are found.

Barefoot on dreams, the journey's bout,
Embracing what the soul without,
The untrodden route, a quest for more,
Through veils unseen, its secrets pour.

Into the Enigma

Beneath a sky of velvet night,
Where constellations weave their light,
A doorway stands, with secrets braced,
Into the enigma, hearts effaced.

Each star a clue to threads unwound,
In cosmic dance, no tethered bound,
A riddle spoken in the dark,
Where silence sings and echoes hark.

Through veils of dew and timeless mist,
With lips unkissed and fears dismissed,
A journey dropped in patterns bright,
Unknown wonders flood the sight.

Every heartbeat syncs with stars,
In the enigma, near and far,
A passage through the vast unknown,
Where dreams alight on destinies sown.

The heavens whisper ancient lore,
In cosmic tapestries galore,
To venture here is to become,
A part of all, yet part of one.

In the Quiet Wilderness

In the quiet wilderness, where shadows talk,
The trees keep secrets, in ancient bark,
Where rivers whisper, in gentle flow,
And silence tells what few may know.

The rustling leaves in whispered tone,
Convey a language all their own,
Each breath confirms life's hidden thread,
Where solitude and soul are wed.

Among the pines and mossy stone,
A haven where the world's unknown,
In quietude, the spirit mends,
And nature's touch makes amends.

The twilight spreads its purple sheen,
Beneath the boughs, a realm serene,
Where time stands still, and dreams compose,
A refuge where the quiet grows.

In every branch, in every breeze,
A song of ancient mysteries,
In the quiet wilderness, hearts find,
A deeper truth, by stars aligned.

Tracks in Secrecy

Beneath the moon’s soft silver sheen,
Where secrets lie in fields unseen,
Tracks in secrecy, a tale unfolds,
Through winding paths, where night beholds.

Each footfall, soft, in shadows cast,
A whisper of the moments past,
Through forest deep and meadow wide,
Where ancient echoes softly bide.

The midnight air with secrets rife,
In every crease, unfolding life,
A journey carved in whispered care,
Tracks in secrecy leading where?

In veils of dusk, in cloaks of mist,
The hidden paths are softly kissed,
By moonlight's grace, the truth is caught,
In steps so soft, with dreams inwrought.

Through secret trails and silent plea,
A dance of shadows, wild and free,
Tracks in secrecy, paths unfurl,
And bind the night in mystery’s twirl.

Shrouded Pathways

Through mist and rolling fog they wind,
A tangled maze of thoughts confined,
Where shadows play and secrets lie,
Beneath an ever-watching sky.

Their curves and turns, a cryptic dance,
Invite, enshroud, confuse at glance,
Footfalls silent, whispers near,
In every corner, fate unclear.

Lost within their veiled embrace,
Time itself seems to lose pace,
Dim-lit lanterns mark the gloom,
Of pathways wrapped in twilight's loom.

Dappled light, a fleeting guide,
Amongst the trees where shadows bide,
Echoed calls from realm unknown,
Lead the way through paths overgrown.

In shrouded pathways' mystic hold,
Tales of old and new unfold,
Revealed to those who seek, who yearn,
In every twist and every turn.

Secrets Beneath the Canopy

Beneath the canopy so wide,
Where beings of the woodland hide,
A world of whispers, soft as breeze,
Dwells in shadows 'neath the trees.

In dappled light, the secrets glow,
Amongst the roots they twist and grow,
The forest's breath, a gentle hum,
Of ancient stories yet to come.

Each leaf a page, each branch a tale,
Of love and loss, of breeze and gale,
The hidden life within the wood,
Unseen, yet always understood.

Creatures small in cryptic dance,
In ceaseless play, in timeless trance,
Guardians of a realm concealed,
To those who seek, its truths revealed.

Deep within, the heartbeats merge,
With whispered secrets on the verge,
Of being known to those who hear,
The murmurs of the forest, clear.

Enigmatic Forest

The forest speaks in riddles low,
With songs that only old winds know,
Its boughs entwined in silent quest,
Of mysteries that never rest.

Soft footsteps tread on ancient ground,
Where secrets whisper without sound,
A world of green and shadowed dread,
Where time is but a thread to shred.

In every leaf a hidden word,
From ages past, a voice unheard,
Beneath the canopy's dark mien,
Lie dreams of lands yet unseen.

Twilight settles, shadows leap,
From hidden haunts where phantoms sleep,
In the stillness of the night,
The forest breathes a hallowed light.

Here amidst the timeless trees,
Echoes drift upon the breeze,
Of the enigmatic tales it keeps,
In roots and skies and mystic deeps.

Night’s Unseen Corridors

When daylight fades to twilight's kiss,
And shadows dance in moonlit bliss,
The night unveils its secret doors,
To walk down unseen corridors.

Stars alight the velvet shroud,
A silent world without the crowd,
Whispers echo in the air,
As dreams awaken, unaware.

Each path a tale of the unknown,
In labyrinths by starlight sown,
Nocturnal beings softly glide,
Along these passages, they abide.

The moon’s soft beam a gentle guide,
Through corridors so vast and wide,
Where silence reigns, and mysteries flow,
In night’s embrace, the secrets glow.

Through dreams and thoughts, the night reveals,
A world where dark and quiet heals,
These unseen corridors unfold,
Their silent stories, dark and bold.

Dark Pine Allegory

In the hush of dark pine whispers,
Shadows cast by ancient figures,
Lost within of endless histories,
Silent tales of yore enshroud.

Mystic needles, green and swaying,
Guarding secrets, never saying,
Labyrinthine pathways playing,
Echoes through the silent shroud.

Moon cut crescents softly gleaming,
Through dark branches gently streaming,
Weaving dreams that seem like teeming,
With the legends of the past.

Graves of whispers, somber sighing,
'Neath the pines where heroes' lying,
In the stillness, undenying,
Time itself must bow at last.

Evergreen these silent sentries,
Hold the woods in darkest tendries,
Untold stories, endless entries,
Bound by roots that hold the cast.

Nature’s Labyrinth

In the heart of nature’s maze,
Winding paths of leafy haze,
Twisting through the green amaze,
Find the soul amidst the trees.

Whispers dance on morning dew,
Hidden shades of every hue,
Labyrinths where life is new,
Journey's end will bring release.

Vines that twine in secret arcs,
Guide the steps and leave their marks,
Through the wild, these ancient sparks,
Nature’s lore and mystery.

Paths that wind in endless trace,
Journeys lost and found in grace,
Nature’s breaths and time’s embrace,
In the forest’s melody.

Every step a story told,
Through the greens and paths of gold,
In the labyrinth they unfold,
Flights of nature’s wild decree.

Ethereal Valleys

Far beyond the rolling hills,
Whispering winds, the air it fills,
With a song of timeless thrills,
Ethereal valleys call.

Morning mists in softest cloud,
Veil the earth in gentle shroud,
Silent rays in beams endowed,
Dawn's serene and tranquil thrall.

Rivers weave through silent lands,
Crafted by unknown, gentle hands,
Echoes through the astral bands,
Dreamlike whispers gently fall.

Blossoms dance in twilight’s glow,
Windswept whispers from below,
Carving tales where soft winds blow,
In those valleys, hear the call.

Moonlit paths through valleys run,
Underneath the setting sun,
In those realms where dreams are spun,
Ethereal dreams for all.

Haunted Woods' Journey

Step into the woods of lore,
Where echoes linger, shadows pour,
Phantom whispers from the core,
Haunted paths where legends play.

Leaves like whispers underfoot,
Guide the heart through every nook,
Tales of wraiths and whispers took,
Bygone spirits find their way.

Moonlight spills on quiet glades,
Softly shifts through wooded shades,
Ghostly forms in twilight's fades,
Haunted nights and spectral day.

Creaking branches, spectral sighs,
Veil the truth in masquerades,
Through the dark where silence lies,
Spirit tales through trees convey.

Journey where the spirits dwell,
In the woods with tales to tell,
In those shadows, magic's spell,
Haunted woods, where echoes stay.

Beyond the Familiar

Beyond the hills of comfort’s reign,
Lies a world untouched by strain.
In lands unknown, free from the chain,
Adventure’s heart shall ever gain.

Stars mark paths in skies untamed,
Through winds and storms, our spirits flamed.
New horizons brightly named,
In realms where dreams are framed.

Eyes wide open, hearts apart,
We journey on from the start.
Into the vast, where visions chart,
The quest for truth, an unyielding art.

Mysterious Voyages

Beneath the silver moonlit skies,
The ship sails on with whispered cries,
Each wave a tale, each star a guide,
Upon the sea, we slowly glide.

Through mist and fog, the shores unseen,
In dreams we chase what might have been,
An odyssey of hidden lore,
With every turn, we seek for more.

The compass spins with secrets old,
In waters deep and stories told,
Ghostly whispers fill the night,
Guiding hearts towards the light.

A journey vast where time stands still,
Through tempests fierce and calm so chill,
Unknown destinations in sight,
With courage bold, we face the flight.

In silent awe of ocean's grace,
We wander on in soft embrace,
Towards horizons dark and wide,
Where mysteries and wonders bide.

Echoes in the Undergrowth

Whispers weave through moss and fern,
In secret groves where shadows turn.
Beneath the canopy, hearts learn,
The ancient songs that always yearn.

Crickets play a nighttime tune,
Owls converse beneath the moon.
Paths of mystery catch our swoon,
In the forest's soft commune.

Leaves like whispers touch the ground,
Silent footsteps make no sound.
In twilight's arms, we're gently bound,
In echoes that forever resound.

The Wolf's Secret Route

In shadows deep, the wolf resides,
Through ancient woods, in silent strides,
With eyes that gleam in moonlit night,
He travels paths beyond our sight.

Among the trees, a hidden trail,
Where leaves and whispers tell their tale,
A journey kept from human kin,
A world within, a world to spin.

Through crystal brooks and valleys low,
Where starlit secrets softly glow,
The wolf, a phantom in the mist,
In nature's arms, by dreams, he's kissed.

With paw-prints light on mossy ground,
No trace remains, no single sound,
He wanders through the night's embrace,
A guardian of this mystic space.

The wind may howl, the forest sighs,
Yet on he treads with keen bright eyes,
On secret routes and hidden ways,
The wolf, unseen, through nights and days.

Into the Uncharted

Through pastures green and skies so wide,
We venture forth with hearts as guide,
Into the lands where maps unmade,
A realm of dreams and sunlight's shade.

Beyond the hills and rivers bend,
Where tales unknown and wonders blend,
Each step we take, a new world born,
In dawn's soft light, a fresh new morn.

No charts to lead, no stars to claim,
We walk with courage, hearts aflame,
Into horizons vast and bright,
With trust in paths that feel so right.

The mountains call, the deserts sing,
In each unknown, a hope they bring,
For in the unmarked paths we tread,
We find ourselves where none have led.

Through mist and rain, through sunlit gold,
With every step, brave stories told,
Into the uncharted we shall roam,
And find, in wilds, our truest home.

Whispers of the Wild

In forest depths where shadows lay,
Where ancient lives and secrets play,
The whispers of the wild are heard,
In rustling leaves and wings of bird.

The trees that tower, old and wise,
Speak quietly to clouded skies,
Their branches weave a soft embrace,
A mystic chant, a hidden grace.

The rivers sing a lullaby,
To creatures passing softly by,
A melody of life and time,
In nature’s choir, pure and sublime.

Through meadows green and mountains tall,
The spirits of the wild call,
In every bloom and breeze we feel,
The whispering wild, so bright, so real.

With every step in nature's spell,
A story woven, hearts compel,
To listen close and understand,
The voices of this ancient land.

Obscured Footprints

Lost in the sands of time we tread,
Silent stories left unread.
In deserts vast where dreams have fled,
Footprints drift, by winds are led.

Shadows fall on dunes of gold,
Secrets ancient, tales untold.
In twilight's breath, the night unfolds,
A dance of memories, brave and bold.

Through the vast expanse we roam,
With every step, closer to home.
Yet paths obscure in dust and loam,
Leave traces fragile as sea foam.

Misty Woodland Treks

Through veils of morning’s hush, we glide,
Beneath the towering trees abide.
Whispers of ancient bark and vine,
Guiding souls to paths divine.

Fern and thistle kiss the air,
In secret nooks, we share our care.
A canopy of dreams unfurls,
Sheltering this world of pearls.

Footsteps soft on mossy ground,
In this embrace, peace is found.
Crisp leaves echo tales of old,
Stories in the mist retold.

The whispering brook runs clear and bright,
Reflecting fractured shards of light.
In this place, our spirits mend,
Misty woodland, timeless friend.

In shadows deep, in sunlight’s play,
An ancient dance we tread each day.
Where forest green and dreams converge,
On misty treks, our hearts emerge.

Ghosts of Pine Paths

Beneath the canopy of green,
Whispers of the past are seen.
Ghostly figures, soft and light,
Wander through the silent night.

Pine needles carpet ancient ways,
Echoes of forgotten days.
The breeze, a messenger of old,
Brings haunting tales yet to be told.

In the stillness of the wood,
Ancestral spirits understood.
Their stories etched in bark and stone,
Where trees and shadows interlace.

Mist tangled in the branches low,
Secrets in the moonlight glow.
With every step, the past awakes,
And through the pines, the present shakes.

Among the pines, where spirits dwell,
Time dissolves, with tales to tell.
In these woods, a bridge in rhyme,
Between the worlds, and through all time.

Under A Hidden Sky

Beneath the boughs of silent pine,
A secret sky, where stars align.
Hidden from the world's keen sight,
Glows gently in the soft twilight.

In twilight's cloak, we find our path,
Away from time's relentless wrath.
Each star, a whisper from afar,
Guides us like some cosmic scar.

In the stillness, hearts converse,
With the universe, we rehearse.
Dreams and wishes, pure and high,
Dance beneath that hidden sky.

Leaves above, like fragments, part,
To show the sky, to ease the heart.
In the sacred quiet night,
We find our solace, soft and bright.

Underneath that sky concealed,
All of nature's love revealed.
There, beneath the stars, we lie,
Dreaming under a hidden sky.

Forests of the Mind

Within the vast and verdant scope,
Our minds explore, in endless hope.
Forests dense with thoughts and dreams,
Flowing like the mountain streams.

Ideas bloom in shaded nooks,
Ephemeral as the babbling brooks.
In the silence of the trees,
Whispered thoughts drift with ease.

Each tree a memory, standing tall,
Each branch a path that beckons all.
Wandering these inner woods,
We find where wisdom long has stood.

With every thought, a leaf unfurls,
A story told in verdant swirls.
Beneath the canopy of thought,
Truths and insights are subtly taught.

In these mental forests bright,
We find ourselves in darkest night.
Among the trees, both mind and soul,
We wander, seeking to be whole.

Paths diverge within our sight,
In forests vast where dreams take flight.
Through mind and spirit, wild yet kind,
We navigate these woods refined.

The Lone Expedition

Through silent peaks, where echoes lie,
A lone traveler meets the sky.
Mountains high and valleys sigh,
In solitude, the spirits fly.

Glacial rivers carve the stone,
Through lands unseen, the path unknown.
Each step a verse in nature's tone,
The soul in woods has never known.

Cold winds whisper tales of old,
While stars like lanterns faintly hold.
Guiding through the nights so cold,
To places where brave hearts unfold.

Echoes in the Pines

In the forest deep and old,
Whispers haunt the silent air,
Tales of secrets left untold,
Echoes reaching everywhere.

Pines stand tall, their shadows play,
Dancing light on needles green,
Songs of dusk at close of day,
Whistling winds where dreams convene.

Owls watch with wise old eyes,
As twilight wraps the earth around,
Echoes rise beneath the skies,
Every heart begins to pound.

Footsteps lost in ages past,
Ghostly memories now unfold,
In the pines their spells are cast,
Touching souls with fingers cold.

In the forest deep and old,
Echoes live in whispered voice,
Silent stories softly told,
Leaving hearts with silent choice.

Hidden Forest Tales

Beneath the canopy so dense,
Stories weave with every breeze,
Every leaf a narrative,
Whispered by the trees' decrees.

Mossy paths that twist and turn,
Shade the secrets down below,
Every step a tale to learn,
Of the lives that come and go.

Shadows speak in ancient tongues,
History in muted hues,
Every creature old or young,
Holds a lore one can't refuse.

Brook's soft murmur tells a tale,
Of a world unseen, unknown,
Hidden stories richly frail,
In the forest overgrown.

Beneath the canopy so dense,
Legends form a mystic veil,
Forest whispers, we commence,
Listening to the hidden tale.

Unseen Journeys

Paths that stretch beyond the eye,
Hidden by the twilight's grace,
Journeys where the spirits fly,
Touching every sacred place.

Footfalls light on ancient ground,
Tracing steps of those before,
Unseen journeys lost, then found,
In the whispers evermore.

Through the fog, the way unclear,
Guided by a silent song,
Heartbeats fill the void with cheer,
Travels where the souls belong.

Veils of mystery entwine,
Roads that never meet the end,
In the forest, age divine,
Journeys blend and then transcend.

Paths that stretch beyond the eye,
Mystic realms of endless night,
Unseen truths that never die,
Guiding souls toward the light.

Mysteries of the Dark Wood

Within the shadows, lost and deep,
Mysteries of the dark wood hide,
Secrets that the night would keep,
Wherein restless spirits bide.

Branches whisper tales of yore,
Creaking with the winds of time,
Through the mist their voices pour,
Chanting in a mystic rhyme.

Hollows echo silent screams,
Wanderers who lost their way,
Dreaming now in endless dreams,
Bound to night, devoid of day.

Starlight filters thin and cold,
Casting beams that barely pierce,
From this realm where stories're told,
Of the fate that nature steers.

Within the shadows, dark and deep,
Mysteries the wood bestows,
Secrets that the night would keep,
In its silent, solemn prose.

Wandering Wildly

In paths where shadows freely sprawl,
We wander through the trees so tall,
With every step, a secret calls,
Leaves whisper, stories enthrall.

The wind, our unseen guiding friend,
Through fields of green, the whispers send,
Into the horizon, paths extend,
In wandering, our hearts transcend.

Through meadows where the flowers bloom,
Underneath the silver moon,
We chase the stars, evade the gloom,
Our spirits free, our wonder's tune.

In forests deep, where silence reigns,
We leave behind our worldly chains,
In nature's lap, no losses, gains,
Just pure embrace, where wildness reigns.

With every breath and every sigh,
We merge with earth, the ground, the sky,
In nature's fold, no questions why,
Just living free, until we fly.

Mountains and Shadows

Across the ridge, the shadows play,
As sunlight fades, the end of day,
In twilight's hush, the mountains sway,
Majestic giants, strong and gray.

The peaks that kiss the heavens high,
Where eagles soar and dare to fly,
Beneath their watch, the valleys lie,
A canvas framed by sky and sigh.

The streams that carve the hardened stone,
With whispers soft, a gentle tone,
Through ages past, their paths well known,
In mountains' heart, where secrets groan.

By starlit nights, the shadows deep,
A silence vast, a peaceful sleep,
In mountains' fold, our dreams to keep,
Where whispers of the night do creep.

The dawn will rise, the shadows chase,
As light returns to soft embrace,
In mountains' might, we find our place,
In nature's arms, a timeless grace.

Stealthy Paws

In moonlit nights where secrets hide,
The forest whispers far and wide,
With stealthy paws, the shadows glide,
A silent dance by nature's guide.

The night is young, the hunters prowl,
Through forests deep, the mystic howl,
With eyes agleam, and spirits foul,
They trace the prey, without avowal.

Each stealthy step, a ghostly plight,
Through underbrush and dark of night,
With patience keen, their senses tight,
In silence, they pursue the flight.

The forest breathes, a heavy sigh,
As stealthy paws in shadows lie,
In nature's game, where dreams can die,
Yet in the hunt, the heart's reply.

The dawn will break, the night will wane,
The forest wakes to life's refrain,
In day's embrace, the shadows' pain,
Yet stealthy paws will come again.

Intrigue of the Pines

Among the pines where secrets dwell,
The needles weave a mystic spell,
Each passing breeze, a tale to tell,
In whispers soft, the pines rebel.

Their fragrance sweet, the air they fill,
With ancient lore, the time stands still,
In shadows deep, the heart's free will,
By pines' embrace, the soul they thrill.

The sunlit beams through branches play,
An intricate dance, the light array,
In pines' domain, both night and day,
A mystery that leads astray.

From roots below to canopy's crest,
The pines retain their silent quest,
In solitude, they stand confessed,
Their secrets kept, the heart caressed.

As twilight falls, the pines remain,
In steadfastness, through joy and pain,
Their whispers call, a sweet refrain,
The intrigue of the pines, our gain.